1

Today Hamid could hardly wait to get to school.
He was going to tell his class about his stay in
Malaysia. For once, his mother didn't have to tell
him to hurry.

"This is your big day, Hamid," she said.
"Do you have all your pictures?"

"They're in my backpack," said Hamid.

"Well, have a good time!" said his mother.

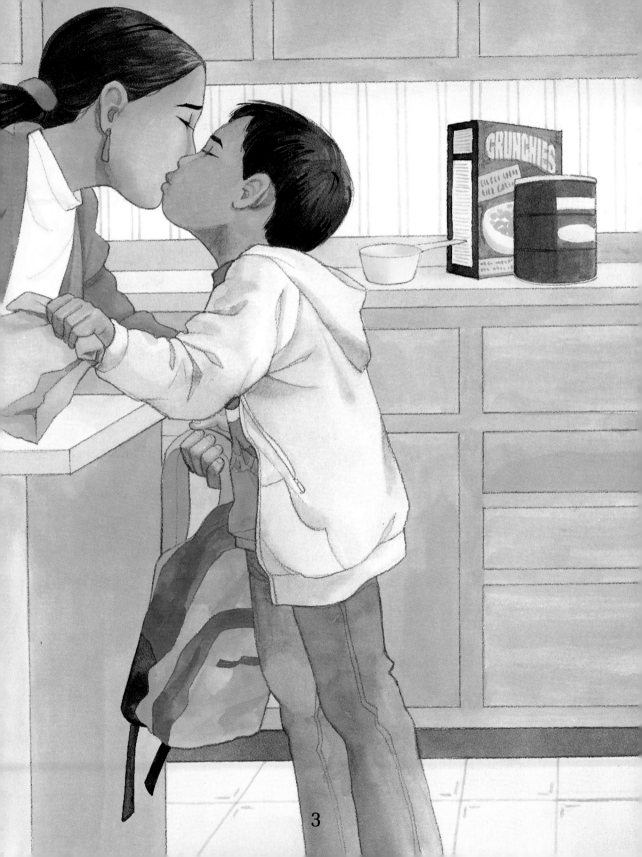

At school, Hamid could hardly wait until it was
time to tell about his trip.

Finally, Ms. Cole said, "Now Hamid is going to tell
us about Malaysia. First, will you show us where
Malaysia is, Hamid?"

"Malaysia is in Asia. Part of it is on an island
and the other part is here, where my grandmother
and grandfather live. It's much hotter in Malaysia
than it is here."

"What do they do for work?" asked Sara.

"Grandmother and Grandfather are farmers,"
said Hamid. "They grow most of their own food.
They live near the water, so they get fish, too."

"What kind of house do they live in?" said Bob.

"It's made of wood, and the roof is made of grass," said Hamid. "And it's up off the ground. Sometimes the farm animals stay under the house."

"Come on!" said Matt. "You're making that up!"

"No, I'm not," said Hamid. "I know it sounds funny, but I'll show you a picture that I took."

Hamid showed the picture. "This is where my grandmother and grandfather live," he said. "You can see some goats under the house."

"WOW," said everyone.

"Tell us more about Malaysia," said Matt.

"I will," said Hamid. "Just let me find the other pictures."

Finally Hamid said, "And here's the best part
of all. My grandmother and grandfather took me
to a place where we saw fish that came out of
the water and walked!"

"Fish that did *what?*" said Matt. "Come on!
You're making that up!"

"No, I'm not," said Hamid. "I'll show you."

Hamid showed some pictures.

"These fish are called Mudskippers," he said.

"They look so funny!" said Ed.

"Why do they come out of the water?" asked Jill.

"To find food," said Hamid. "They get flies from the air, and snails from the wet dirt. They lay their eggs in the wet dirt, too."

"How do they walk?" asked Nicky.

"They push with their fins and then they make a little jump," said Hamid. "It's so funny to watch them."

"How long can they stay out of water?"
asked Lynn.

"They can stay out for a long time," said Hamid,
"but they always keep pretty close to the water."

"Well, I saw your pictures and I know you took them," said Matt. "But I still think you're making it all up!"

Everyone laughed, even Hamid.

Then Ms. Cole said, "Thank you, Hamid. That was great! I wish we could all go with you to Malaysia the next time!"